LIVING WITH
LADY MACBETH

ACT NOW PLAYS

Series editor: Peter Rowlands
Founding editor: Andrew Bethell

LIVING WITH LADY MACBETH
Rob John

CAMBRIDGE
UNIVERSITY PRESS

Published by the Press Syndicate of the University of Cambridge
The Pitt Building, Trumpington Street, Cambridge CB2 1RP
40 West 20th Street, New York, NY 10011–4211, USA
10 Stamford Road, Oakleigh, Victoria 3166, Australia

First published 1992

Printed in Great Britain by Greenshires Print Ltd, Kettering,
Northamptonshire

A catalogue record for this book is available from the British Library

ISBN 0 521 42507 7 paperback

Performance
For permission to give a public performance of *Living with Lady
Macbeth* please write to Permissions Department, Cambridge
University Press, The Edinburgh Building, Shaftesbury Road,
Cambridge CB2 2RU.

Cover photograph by Chris Loukes, the Far East Theatre Company.

GE

ABOUT THE PLAY

Living with Lady Macbeth is not a realistic play in terms of its settings and its shape. It flies backwards and forwards in time and presents the central character's dreams and fantasies in a way that a more realistic play could not. I hope, however, that Lily herself *is* realistic. I think that there are millions of Lilys in the world. They're the people who you hardly ever notice, the ones who never get into the in-crowd, who are thought to be dull, unattractive, untalented and totally ordinary. Perhaps we all have days when we feel like Lily and perhaps we too dream of one day doing something remarkable and proving everybody wrong.

I'd also like to say something about Shakespeare. When I was at school I thought that Shakespeare was impossible to understand and incredibly boring. Then, one day, a brilliant teacher switched on the light for me and showed me what I'd been missing. I've been hooked ever since. I defy anyone to watch Lady Macbeth in full flow and find her boring. I've tried to find a way to say this in *Living with Lady Macbeth* but I've got to admit that the best lines in my play are by Shakespeare.

CHARACTERS

LILY MORGAN
A large clumsy girl who has spent her life trying to please people and to be nice. Everybody thinks that Lily is very ordinary and rather dull. They are all wrong.

MON (MONICA)
Lily's best friend. She peers crossly at the world through thick glasses and knows that people laugh at her. She is intensely loyal to Lily.

MOTHER
A comfortable and caring woman who makes soft toys and thanks her lucky stars that Lily is so dull and ordinary because she believes that dull and ordinary girls are safer.

BARRY
Lily's boyfriend. A deeply boring and earnest young man prone to wearing knitted cardigans and sensible shoes.

ALEX
Lily's brother. Alex is bright, confident and frighteningly good at Maths, Physics and karate.

MS BEVIS
A young trendy and intensely enthusiastic teacher.

SUZANNE PORTER
LORRAINE FERGUSON
CAROLINE PRITCHETT
GAIL BENTLEY
STEPHANIE BOYCE
The audience see these five move and think as one. They operate like a sinister machine in their perfect school uniforms. They turn their heads, and laugh in unison and even finish each other's sentences. In Lily's mind they are beautiful, intelligent and effortlessly successful – in other words, the enemy.

MACBETH
Tall, brooding and wild-looking. He comes equipped with tartan cloaks and several murderous-looking knives.

FIRST PRODUCTION

The play was first performed in March 1988 by the Far East Youth Theatre Company at Paston Sixth Form College in Norfolk. The same cast performed the play at the Edinburgh Fringe Festival later that year. They were:

LILY MORGAN   Penny Killow
MON   Zowie Poynter
MOTHER   Kate Dimock
BARRY   Owen Evans
ALEX   Max Hunt
MS BEVIS   Sarah Elsegood
SUZANNE PORTER   Jo Falla
LORRAINE FERGUSON   Tessa Kelly
CAROLINE PRITCHETT   Alexis Keegan
GAIL BENTLEY   Robyn Rockingham
STEPHANIE BOYCE   Sam Gernon
MACBETH   Chris Rundle

STAGE DIRECTIONS

There are two kinds of directions in this playscript. Those in **bold type** provide information that is essential to an understanding of what is happening in the play at the time. For a play-reading, these should be read by a separate reader.

Those in *italic type* are less essential stage directions and offer suggestions to assist with a production of the play onstage. In a reading they are best not read out as they will hamper the flow of the play, although those who are reading may find that some of these instructions offer help with the interpretation of their lines.

An empty stage. The only set is a table, a chair and a raised area upstage right. As houselights dim the cast enter and disperse about the set, facing the audience. As lights go up we hear the cast whispering in unison the lines from *Macbeth* whilst a solo voice sings the chorus from 'Lavender's Blue'.

'When shall we three meet again?
In thunder, lightning, or in rain?
When the hurlyburly's done,
When the battle's lost and won.
That will be ere the set of sun.
Where the place?
Upon the heath.
There to meet with . . .
Macbeth!'

'Lavender's blue, dilly dilly,
Lavender's green;
You will be king dilly dilly,
I will be queen.'

As the cast move slowly to the sides of the stage (the FIVE GIRLS grouping together on the raised area) we hear a lone piper. LILY MORGAN is left alone centre stage. MACBETH, a traditionally costumed figure obviously Shakespearean and clearly Scottish, enters upstage of Lily and gently touches her cheek as he slowly passes her. MONICA enters in towelling robe, swimming hat and goggles. Lily and the Five are wearing identical school uniforms. During the following scene Lily hands Monica her uniform and Monica wrestles it on under her robe. Lily is a large cumbersome girl. Monica is small, bird-like and wears thick glasses.

MON   It'll be crap. School plays are always crap.

LILY   When we saw it . . . When we went to see it . . . it made my skin creep.

MON   Your skin creep?

LILY   Yeah.

MON   Didn't make mine creep.

LILY   It was wonderful . . . She was wonderful.

MON   Made my bum ache.

LILY   I'm going to be in it.

MON   You?

LILY   Why not?

MON   Well . . . They've got Suzanne Porter and all that lot.

LILY   So?

MON   They've all been in loads of plays. They're brilliant. Well, some of them are. Stephanie Boyce is brilliant.

LILY   Stephanie Boyce hasn't got the power for Lady Macbeth.

MON   You're not thinking of Lady Macbeth are you?

LILY   All the time. I think about her all the time.

MON   Lady Macbeth?

LILY   Lady Macbeth.

MON   Oh . . .

LILY   The wheels are already in motion, Monica.

MON   Are they?

LILY   I saw Bevis about it. I waited outside her room after I saw the notice. I said . . .

(MS BEVIS appears.)

Excuse me, Miss, I was wondering about *Macbeth*.

MS BEVIS   Yes?

LILY   Well, when are the auditions going to be?

MS BEVIS   End of next week, probably. Are you interested, Lily?

LILY   Yes, I am, Miss. I'm very interested actually.

MS BEVIS   Oh . . . You haven't actually acted before, have you?

LILY   No, Miss. That's because I had this job . . . in a shop . . . in the evenings. But I don't do that any more.

MS BEVIS   Well, we'll be looking for strong actresses.

LILY   Yes, I appreciate that, Miss.

MS BEVIS   And particularly people who are reliable and committed.

LILY   Oh, I'm reliable and committed. I mean when I'm committed I'm really committed. And reliable.

MS BEVIS   Yes, I know that, Lily. Well, OK. I'll put your name down.

(MS BEVIS exits.)

LILY   Thanks, Miss . . . and she put my name down. I've started work on it actually.

MON   On Lady Macbeth?

LILY   Yes.

MON   Lily are you sure about this? No one's going to see you as Lady Macbeth . . . are they?

LILY   Monica, don't say that. Don't talk like that. You'll see. Just you wait. (*Lights change.*)

(The voice sings 'Lavender's Blue' as LILY sits on the table reading from a copy of *Macbeth*. As the characters are introduced they move quickly in from the sides of the set to join Lily.)

LILY   'Come, you spirits
That tend on mortal thoughts,
unsex me here . . .'

MOTHER   Lily's very ordinary really. Always was very ordinary. Even as a baby. Apart from being on the large side and unusually clumsy she was very ordinary, which is no bad thing I always say . . . for a girl . . . being ordinary. If they're blessed with brains, then sooner or later they end up looking down their noses at you and if they're pretty then before you know where you are you've got youths in leather jackets sniffing round the garden gate at all hours of the day and night. No, give me a girl like Lily every time. I've never worried about her. Do you know that? I've never lost a moment's sleep over that girl.

LILY   'And fill me, from the crown to the toe, top-full
Of direst cruelty.'

BARRY   I think I might actually be in love with Lily, although I might be wrong. I'm not quite sure what being in love feels like, but I expect I probably am. We've only been seeing each other for about three and a half months so perhaps it's a bit early to be precise on that. What I like about her is (a) she's really bright. Much more clever than me. She's doing A levels and everything and (b) she's got a really good sense of humour. Well, we've got that in common because I'm quite a joker myself. (c) She doesn't ever make an exhibition of herself in the way she behaves or dresses like some girls do. I hate that, and (d) well, she's dependable. You know where you are with her. You feel safe with Lily.

LILY   ' . . . make thick my blood,
Stop up the access and passage to remorse;
That no compunctious visitings of nature
Shake my fell purpose . . .'

ALEX   I don't really think about her that much. We've got nothing in common. We're totally unalike. I mean she's really thick. She's doing A levels in History and English and to do them it's practically a course requirement to be brain-damaged. Where's History and English going to get you then, eh? Now I'm going to sixth form next year to do Maths, Physics and Chemistry 'cos I'm quite technologically minded. Yes, I take after my dad . . . or so people tell me and I suppose she takes after mum. I do weights and karate whereas Lily . . . I don't think that Lily does anything. She just hangs about with Mon . . . The delectable Monica, who was voted this year by the fifth year boys as the sixth form girl they'd least like to . . . you know. And she goes out with Barry . . . (*sings*) Ba – a – ree . . . When I do that at home she goes beserk. No, I don't think about her that much. She's OK, I suppose.

LILY   'Come to my woman's breasts,
And take my milk for gall, you murdering ministers,
Wherever in your sightless substances
You wait on nature's mischief!'

MS BEVIS   Oh she's terribly nice is Lily. A real trier. Not overbright. Reached her peak at GCSE I'd say, but she could
scrape an A level or two. The sort of kid you write 'Has
made the most of her ability' on her report. You know
the sort . . . Single-parent family. Mother's very
supportive. Makes ghastly soft toys for school fêtes.
That sort of thing. She's got a brother in the fifth year.
Now he's bright, so I'm told. Very bright. She worries
about her work. Sweated blood over Gerard Manley
Hopkins, poor kid, but she does her best. Someone told
me she had a boyfriend, which really surprised me
actually, but good for her I thought. Perhaps that'll give
her some confidence. That's what she really needs . . .
confidence.

LILY   ' . . . Come, thick night,
And pall thee in the dunnest smoke of hell,
That my keen knife see not the wound it makes . . .'

THE FIVE   (1) Lily . . . She's alright is Lily (2) I quite like her (1)
GIRLS   I quite like her . . . I didn't say I didn't like her (3) I like
her . . . I mean she's (4) she's alright (5) We haven't got
anything against her (1) she's a bit boring (2) dull . . .
she's dull (3) Yeah, she is a bit (4) She doesn't really try
(5) I mean look at her hair (1) Oh god, her hair (2) That
time at Helen's party (3) Oh yeah (4) It was incredible
(5) was ridiculous (1) And Caroline went up to her and
said (2) What did she say? (3) I can't remember, but it
was hilarious (4) And we all peed ourselves laughing
(5) but she didn't mind (1) Oh no, that's the thing about
Lily (2) she can take a joke (3) Like that time in English
(4) Oh yeah, when she asked Bevis a question . . . What
was it? (5) About Hopkins . . . What was it? (1) Can't
remember, but we just wet ourselves (2) and even Bevis
was smirking (3) and Lily didn't know (4) what we were
laughing about (5) It was so funny . . . (1) No, she's
alright, is Lily (2) She's got Monica (3) Mon (4) Good
old Mon (5) And Barry . . . she's got Barry (1) Oh that
is so weird (2) gruesome (3) totally gross (4) Just
imagine . . . (5) I think he's cute (1) Yes he's cute . . . he's

quite cute (2) He's alright . . . for Lily (*They erupt laughing.*) (3) She's alright . . . (4) Yeah . . . (5) She's alright is Lily.

LILY ' . . . Nor heaven peep through the blanket of the dark, To cry . . .'

MON Lily?

(**The other characters swiftly disperse.**)

LILY What?

MON You still . . .?

LILY What?

MON   . . . working on Lady Macbeth?

LILY Yes.

MON How's it going? One week to go . . . Going alright is it?

LILY It's alright.

MON Good.

LILY It's terrible.

MON Oh.

LILY I can't seem to get through to people what I want to do.

MON Well this is it, Lily. This is what I . . .

LILY My mother.

MON What does she say?

LILY What do you think?

(**MOTHER** appears at the table. **LILY** lurches to centre stage struggling to remember the lines from *Macbeth*.)

LILY 'That which hath made them drunk hath made me bold . . .'

MOTHER I don't think this is very suitable for a school play to be honest, Lily. What made them choose this?

LILY   It's a great play, Mum. 'What hath quenched them . . .'

MOTHER   So you say. I don't see what's so great about it. It's very violent, isn't it?

LILY   Yes, Mum.

MOTHER   And this Lady Macbeth . . . She's a bit . . .

LILY   What?

MOTHER   Well, she's not at all like you, is she?

LILY   Mum, just prompt me, will you?

MOTHER   More of a fiery type I'd say.

LILY   Mum!

MOTHER   Alright. Fire away.

LILY   'What hath given me fire' . . . Sod it . . . Prompt.

MOTHER   Pardon?

LILY   Prompt. When I say prompt . . . you prompt me.

MOTHER   Sorry, where are we?

LILY   'That which hath made them drunk hath made me bold:
What hath quenched them hath given me fire. Hark!
Peace!'
That's it . . . I remember it. 'It was the owl that shrieked,
the fatal bellman whence . . .'

MOTHER   So you didn't need a prompt.

LILY   No, Mum. ' . . . the fatal bellman . . .'

MOTHER   'Which gives the . . .'

LILY   Shut up . . . Sorry. ' . . . the fatal bellman,
which gives the stern'st goodnight. He is about it.
The doors are open; and the surfeited grooms
Do mock their charge with snores: I have drugged their possetts,
That death . . .'

MOTHER   What are possetts? . . . You've drugged their possetts? What are they?

LILY   Um . . . sort of fruit.

MOTHER   Oh.

MON   No they're not.

LILY   What?

MON   Possetts aren't fruit.

LILY   Aren't they?

MOTHER   What sort of fruit?

LILY   Um . . . sort of little greengages.

MOTHER   Oh. Don't sound all that nice, do they?

LILY   Mum, please.

MOTHER   Sorry.

LILY   ' . . . Do mock their charge with snores: I have drugged . . .'

MOTHER   You know who I see doing this?

LILY   Who?

MOTHER   Stephanie Boyce. This is right up her street. Proper little madam she is. I wouldn't trust her as far as I could throw her. I can see her doing all this possett-drugging business with no difficulty. She's a good actress, mind. She'd be very good. Typecast by the look of this, but very good.

LILY   Mum, please!

(MOTHER freezes.)

MON   She's not been too much help then.

LILY   No. Oh she tries, but you can see what she's thinking.

MOTHER   Poor old Lily. Whatever will she think of next. Lady Macbeth for goodness sake.

(MOTHER returns to her position.)

LILY 'Lady Macbeth . . . for goodness sake!' It's what everyone's thinking, isn't it, Mon? Isn't it?

MON I don't know.

LILY It's what Barry thinks.

MON Is it?

(**BARRY** enters.)

BARRY Well can't we go out later when you've done your homework?

LILY I'm not doing homework. I'm learning my speech. I told you.

BARRY Well, we could go over it together. I could help you.

LILY I've got to learn it myself.

BARRY Well, we could discuss it. Talk about the part . . . Discuss the play.

LILY But you don't know the play, Barry.

BARRY How do you know I don't know it? Why do you automatically assume I don't know it?

LILY Well *do* you know it?

BARRY No I don't, actually. But I don't like you assuming I don't know things. I'm not thick.

LILY I know that. I'm sorry. I never said you were thick, Barry.

BARRY You implied . . .

LILY I'm sorry. I'm sorry. I'm a bit wound up.

BARRY That's alright, Lily. I understand.

LILY Alright, let's discuss it.

BARRY Alright.

(**BARRY** freezes.)

MON You discussed *Macbeth* with Barry?

LILY   Why not? He's not thick.

MON   I never said he was.

LILY   Not that thick anyway.

BARRY   So fill me in, Lily. What's this scene all about?

LILY   Right. Macbeth – Thane of Cawdor.

BARRY   A thane is?

LILY   A sort of lord.

BARRY   A sort of lord . . . right.

LILY   He wants to be king and all he's got to do to be king is to kill Duncan . . . the king . . . and then he'll be king.

BARRY   Sounds risky, Lily.

LILY   Exactly . . . exactly. This is the point. This is exactly the point. He's scared. Now, Lady Macbeth . . .

BARRY   Macbeth's wife . . . right.

LILY   Right. Me. I want him to do it. I desperately want him to do it. I want him on that throne.

BARRY   So you'd become queen.

LILY   Exactly. So in this scene I have to convince him to do it.

BARRY   I get the picture. You have to convince him to do it.

LILY   Yes . . . Now Duncan is staying overnight at Macbeth's castle.

BARRY   What? At your place?

LILY   Right. So all Macbeth has to do is nip upstairs and stab Duncan with a knife (*hands Barry a knife*) whilst he's asleep.

BARRY   But he's scared.

LILY   So I insult his manhood.

BARRY   Do you?

LILY And I question his love for me.

BARRY Oh.

LILY And remind him of his promise.

BARRY What promise?

LILY He promised to do it.

BARRY When?

LILY In Act I, Scene 5.

BARRY Oh. You didn't tell me about that.

LILY Well he did. I tell him to screw his courage to the sticking place and go and do it.

BARRY But he's still scared.

LILY Right. So I tell him no one will suspect because we'll smear the faces of the sleeping grooms with blood so everyone'll think it's them.

BARRY Grooms? What grooms?

LILY Duncan's got grooms up there with him.

BARRY Has he? . . . Why?

LILY I don't know. Kings always have grooms handy. At any time they may need to saddle up and ride off to administer the affairs of state.

BARRY But what if they wake up?

LILY We'll drug their possetts.

BARRY Their what?

LILY Possetts. They're like scones. Little curranty scones.

MON No they're not, Lily.

LILY Shut up, Mon!

BARRY So people are expected to believe that these grooms have nipped into whatshisname's bedroom . . .

LILY   Duncan's bedchamber.

BARRY   And stabbed the king. Then presumably knackered by the exertions of the crime they've gone back to their own bedchambers and gone to sleep, still clutching the murder weapons and failing to notice that their faces are smeared with royal blood.

MON   He's got a point there, Lily.

LILY   Shut up Mon . . . Yes, that's basically the plan.

BARRY   It'd never work, Lil. No one'd fall for it. It's got to be a fit-up.

LILY   It'd work. It does work.

BARRY   Are you sure you've got this right?

LILY   Of course I'm sure.

BARRY   Well I can't see it.

LILY   It's in the book! They do it. She does it!

BARRY   Well, I don't like the sound of it, Lil.

LILY   Well, you don't have to like the sound of it. It's got nothing to do with you. (*long pause*)

BARRY   Well, I think you should think twice before getting involved in this type of thing.

MON   What did he mean 'this type of thing'?

LILY   That's what I said . . . What do you mean 'this type of thing'? And he said . . .

BARRY   It's not you Lily . . . You're too . . .

LILY   What? . . . I'm too what, Barry?

BARRY   You're too nice.

MON   And what did you say?

LILY   Get out.

BARRY   What?

LILY   Out . . . out . . . out.

(BARRY returns to his position.)

Are you listening to me, Mon? Are you listening?

MON   Yes.

LILY   When I was a kid we used to have this thing in our house
that when you got a loose eyelash . . . if you found one
. . . you could put it on your hand and blow it away and
make a wish. You weren't supposed to tell anybody
what your wish was, but my mum would always ask. I
don't know why. Maybe she wanted to check our wishes
were healthy and appropriate. One day, when I was
about eight, I had an eyelash and I blew it and made a
wish. And mum, as always, said . . .

MOTHER   Come on, Lily. You tell Mummy. What did you wish
for?

LILY   And I said, 'I wish that all the other little girls and boys
in the world would be as lucky as me and have enough to
eat and live in peace and have a mummy who loved
them.' And my mum hugged me and said . . .

MOTHER   Oh Lily. That's so typical of you. You're such a funny
little lump. I do love you. You know, you haven't got a
nasty thought in your head.

LILY   Of course what I'd really wished was that my brother,
my beautiful fair-haired, gifted, lovable little brother
would break his back in an accident and have to spend
the rest of his life in a wheelchair . . . That's the sort of
person I am, Mon. But they don't know that . . .
Nobody knows.

(A voice sings 'Lavender's Blue', as MACBETH walks slowly
towards LILY. During this section Macbeth stands behind Lily
with his arms wrapped around her. She leans her head back into
him, her eyes shut. The characters appear on cue by either
advancing from their 'waiting' positions or through the use of
independently lit areas.)

MOTHER   I really don't know what you're thinking of. You've got enough on your plate without taking up acting.

BARRY   Now, I can see you doing Juliet . . . in *Romeo and Juliet*, I mean. But not Lady Macbeth . . . I mean she's mad, Lil.

MS BEVIS   What we'll be looking for in all the female parts is strength. Witches, Lady Macduff and, above all, Lady Macbeth herself. The key is power. That's what we'll be looking for.

ALEX   You must be joking, Lily. You're not going to get involved with that lot. They're a bunch of total . . .

THE FIVE GIRLS   (1) Lily Morgan? (2) No (3) She can't be (4) She has (5) She's signed up for it (1) I don't believe it (2) What . . . Lily! (3) God, how embarrassing.

ALEX   I saw the film and when she goes mad she takes off all her clothes and staggers about in the nude. It's in the script. She has to. I wouldn't mind seeing Stephanie Boyce do that, but not you, Lily.

MS BEVIS   Have you actually done any acting at all, Lily? No? I thought not. There's an awful lot of experienced people reading for the parts. It's going to be tough competition.

THE FIVE GIRLS   (1) Someone's got to tell her (2) It's ridiculous (3) She's never been in anything before (4) Can you imagine it? (5) Someone's got to tell her.

BARRY   I don't know how you think you're going to find the time to do your studying . . . and this play . . . and see me. Something'll have to go.

(MACBETH gently kisses LILY.)

And another thing, Lily.

(She is staring after MACBETH as he slowly departs.)
You've started acting very oddly since this whole business started. *Very* oddly, in my opinion.

(The lights change. LILY gently sings 'Lavender's Blue' to herself.)

LILY   Three days to go, Mon.

(**MON** appears.)

MON   Yes.

LILY   'She is a woman, her eye fixed on the shadow of her solitary ambition.' You know who wrote that?

MON   Why are you doing this, Lily?

LILY   Coleridge. Samuel Taylor Coleridge. I really like that. 'Her eye fixed on the shadow of her solitary ambition'. It's so true.

MON   Lily, listen . . . Why are you doing this? How come all of a sudden you're so hell bent on being Lady Macbeth? . . . People are laughing at you, Lily.

LILY   Laughing?

MON   Well, not everybody. People think it's odd, that's all.

LILY   And what do you think? You think it's odd?

MON   No . . . A bit. It's not like you. You don't want to be part of all that stuff.

LILY   How do you know? How do you know what stuff I want to be part of?

MON   But why, Lily? What's it all for? You won't get it. Why make yourself a laughing stock. You can't possibly get it.

LILY   Why can't I get it?

MON   Alright. You won't get it because there's half a dozen girls in there who've been in every single play they've ever done. And they're good. Some of them are very good. And you won't get it, 'cos Bevis knows them and trusts them . . . (*long pause*) and you won't get it . . . because you're too tall. I mean who've they got to choose Macbeth from? They're all practically midgets. You won't get it. She's already made up her mind.

LILY   She'll change her mind after the audition . . . when she sees me.

MON No, she won't. Auditions are just to make it seem fair. So everyone feels they've had a crack at it. They make their minds up before they even start.

LILY No they don't. When she sees me, she'll . . .

MON Lily, listen to me.

LILY I've learnt it, Mon.

MON What?

LILY Not just a speech for the audition. The whole lot. The whole part. I've learnt it.

MON Oh you haven't.

LILY It's all there. (*Gets book.*) Go on, test me. Anywhere.

MON You won't get it, Lily.

LILY 'Glamis thou art, and Cawdor; and shalt be
What thou art promised. Yet do I fear thy nature:
It is too full of the milk of human kindness,
To catch the nearest . . .'

MON (*shouting*) You won't get it, Lily!

LILY '. . . To catch the nearest way. Thou wouldst be great;
Art not without ambition, but without
The illness . . .'

MON Lily!

LILY '. . . should attend it; what thou wouldst highly . . .'

MON Lily!

LILY '. . . That wouldst thou holily; wouldst not play
false . . .'
WHY WHY NOT . . . Just for once . . . Just for bloody
once why can't it be me?

MON Oh Lily.

(LILY and MON observe this scene in silence.)

ALEX She won't get it.

BARRY   How do you know she won't get it? I suppose you're an expert on Shakespeare now, are you?

ALEX   She won't get it because. Look . . . If you were doing *Macbeth* and you had all that talent to choose from. If you had Suzanne Porter and Lorraine Ferguson and Caroline Pritchett and . . . Who's that dark girl, Mum?

MOTHER   Gail Bentley.

ALEX   Right. Gail Bentley. And as well as these, if you had Stephanie Boyce . . . Oh god . . . Stephanie Boyce. If you had those to choose from you wouldn't pick Lily, would you?

BARRY   But what if they do?

ALEX   Yes . . . Well . . . You don't know Stephanie Boyce. If you knew her then you'd realise they couldn't even consider Lily. Believe me she's wasting her time.

BARRY   Poor Lily. She's going to be devastated.

MOTHER   No she's not. Not Lily. She'll take it on the chin. She doesn't get herself all worked up over things like this. Do you remember the carol-singing competition, Alex?

ALEX   No.

MOTHER   That's all we heard for weeks. She'd set her heart on winning it. 'In the bleak mid-winter lo–o–ong ago.' Over and over again she practised it. We all knew it off by heart by the end of October. And she looked so funny singing it. So serious. Of course she was about a foot taller than all the others. We did laugh. She came seventh and I said, 'Never mind, Lily, you did your best. We're all very proud of you.' And you know, it was like water off a duck's back. She never mentioned it again. She's not a worrier, Lily.

ALEX   This time next week she'll have forgotten all about it

BARRY   But supposing she gets it. That's what's worrying me.

MOTHER   Oh no, love. You can put that right out of your head.

Alex is right. Girls like Lily don't get that sort of thing. Oh no, she's wrong for it.

(The three freeze.)

LILY   Listen to them, Mon. That's me they're talking about. I protest. I protest, Mon. 'Girls like Lily' . . . Makes me want to . . . They taught me to be nice, Mon. Showed me how to be . . . nice. To take the smallest piece of cake . . . to choose the sensible shoes . . . to avoid at all costs making an exhibition of myself . . . to cooperate . . . to accommodate . . . to settle for the good flat solid middle ground of their expectations . . . and to say sorry . . . Sorry, Miss . . . Sorry, Mum . . . You know what really annoys me, Mon? On school trips when all the others used to fight and squabble to sit on the back seat of the coach so they could smoke and make V signs to the passing lorry drivers out the back window . . . where were we, Mon? . . . Where were we? We were up the front sharing our crisps with the teachers . . . that's where we were . . . up the front being nice . . . being good . . . I'll tell you why, too . . . I'll tell you why I was good . . . 'cos I was too bloody scared to be bad, that's why . . . Funny, isn't it . . . when you come to think about it.

(Lighting change. We hear snatches of 'Lavender's Blue' sung in chaotic nightmarish fragments by the whole cast.)

LILY   It's tomorrow, Mon.

MON   I know.

LILY   I've started dreaming about it.

MON   Oh.

LILY   You were in it, actually.

MON   Was I?

LILY   Yes . . . I was standing in a field . . . In my night things and Macbeth was there.

(MACBETH enters.)

It was the real Macbeth.

MON   The real Macbeth?

LILY   Yes. I spoke to him. I remembered the lines.
'Great Glamis! worthy Cawdor!
Greater than both, by the all-hail hereafter!'
You're so tall.

MACBETH   Yes.

LILY   You must be . . .

MACBETH   Six two, six three.

LILY   And I look up into his face . . . I was so afraid you'd be
short.

MACBETH   You afraid? Never . . . my lady. 'Duncan comes here
tonight.'

LILY   'And when goes hence?'

MACBETH   'Tomorrow, as he purposes.'

LILY   'Oh, never
Shall the sun that morrow see!
Your face, my thane, is as a book, where men
May read strange matters.'

(They embrace and he pushes her away.)

MACBETH   Lily!

LILY   'To beguile the time,
Look like the time . . .'

MACBETH   Lily!

LILY   'What ails you my lord? Why do you make such faces
Bear welcome in your eyes' . . . Please.

MACBETH   Lily . . . What are you saying? This isn't like you.

LILY   But it is me.

MACBETH   Lily.

LILY   Don't call me Lily. 'Look like the innocent flower but be the serpent under it.' And then he said . . .

MACBETH   Lily . . . Pull yourself together. You're making an exhibition of yourself.

LILY   And suddenly I felt so ashamed . . . I'm sorry. I'm so sorry. I don't know what came over me . . . And then you were there, Mon, and you said.

MON   'Great Glamis! worthy Cawdor!
Greater than both, by the all-hail hereafter!'

LILY   I tried to stop you, but you walked straight through me.

MACBETH   'My dearest love . . .'

(He takes off MON's glasses and they embrace.)

' . . . Duncan comes here tonight.'

LILY   Mon . . . Stop it. What are you doing?

MON   'And when goes hence?'

MACBETH   'Tomorrow, as he purposes.'

MON   'O, never
Shall the sun that morrow see!
Your face, my thane, is as a book, where men
May read strange matters.'

MS BEVIS   Cut. Thank you, Macbeth. (*Macbeth exits.*) Monica, that was brilliant.

LILY   What?

MS BEVIS   You really are a dark horse, aren't you, Monica?

MON   Yes, Miss.

LILY   She was crap, Miss.

MS BEVIS   An absolute revelation.

MON   Thank you, Miss.

MS BEVIS   You'll accept the part?

LILY   No!

MON   Of course.

LILY   No, Mon! You can't!

MS BEVIS   Lovely. First rehearsal tomorrow lunchtime.

MON   I'll be there, Miss.

MS BEVIS   Just the right blend of evil and power. 'A woman her eye fixed on the shadow of her solitary ambition.'

MON   Coleridge, if I'm not mistaken, Miss.

MS BEVIS   Absolutely. You have been doing your homework. Most impressive.

LILY   I told her that! That's my quote!

MS BEVIS   See you tomorrow, Mon. (*Ms Bevis exits.*)

MON   Yes, Miss.

LILY   No you can't . . . You can't . . . Cut . . . Cut . . .

MON   It was a stupid dream, Lily.

LILY   I know . . . I know.

MON   It won't be me, Lily.

LILY   And it won't be me either . . . will it?

MON   I don't know . . . I don't think so.

LILY   It'll be them, won't it? One of them. It's so obvious. It's so bloody unfair. Always them.

            (Lights up on a tableau of the FIVE GIRLS. They gaze into the distance, a puff of smoke gently floating from the odd mouth here and there.)

LILY   On a wall by the edge of the park they sit. Lunchtimes in the summer. They show their legs and men mowing the grass whistle. They giggle and smoke. I know what they're saying . . . You can tell from a distance . . . By the way they sit . . . By the way that they hold their necks and their arms and their hands and the way they blow their smoke. They're saying . . .

THE FIVE   (1) We feel safe (2) We feel comfortable (3) because we know we're beautiful (4) and that men find us irresistible (5) and we like that (1) because that makes us feel safe (2) and comfortable (3) We're all clever (4) and we're all going to university (5) to read English (1) and French (2) and Social Anthropology (3) and things like that (4) and when we get there (5) men will find us clever (1) and irresistibly attractive (2) and we'll sit about there (3) in languorous groups (4) looking beautiful (5) blowing smoke across (1) manicured (2) ancient (3) lawns (4) Our fathers are all doctors (2) and lawyers (3) and accountants (4) and company directors (5) and lorry drivers (*pause*) (1) But that doesn't matter (2) because she's clever (3) and beautiful (4) and we're happy to be her friend (5) What we won't tolerate are the dumb (1) and dumpy (2) the ugly (3) untrendy (4) girls with anoraks (5) and funny-looking parents (1) with glasses (2) and no 0 levels (3) girls who add nothing to our corporate (5) image and appeal (1) girls (2) in short (3) who are (4) naff (5) like Lily Morgan.

LILY   Sometimes I harbour dark violent thoughts . . . Lady Macbeth style. The way she plots and plans to cut and kill . . . dispose of obstacles, eliminate rivals . . . Blood on her hands. 'My hands are of your colour.' I could kill them, Mon.

MON   Why not?

LILY   You too?

MON   Yes.

LILY   We'd be ruthless, Mon.

MON   'My hands are of your colour.'

LILY   'Come, you spirits'
(*Mon joins in.*) 'That tend on mortal thoughts . . .'

LILY AND   ' . . . unsex us here,
MON   And fill us, from the crown to the toe, top-full
Of direst cruelty.'

LILY   How do you feel, Mon?

MON   Lethal.

LILY   Good.

MON   We'd take them out.

LILY   One by one. 'The sleeping, and the dead.
Are but as pictures; 'tis the eye of childhood
That fears a painted devil.'

MON   Too right. Where would we do it?

LILY   Wherever we felt like, Mon. The mind of evil can
roam . . . wherever it . . . likes. (*Lights start to dim.*)
'Light thickens; and the crow
Makes wing to the rooky wood;
Good things of day begin to droop and drowse,
While night's black agents to their preys do rouse.'

(**BARRY** and **ALEX** appear and crouch in frozen positions
behind **LILY** and **MON**. They will play the additional characters
MR CRABTREE, **LENNIE** the mechanic and the **HANG-
GLIDING INSTRUCTOR**. The following deaths are enacted in
a stylised way, with the cast providing sound effects and the
bodies thrust upwards and held in tableaux for a few seconds at
the moment of death. At each moment of death we hear a tolling
bell and Lily and Mon fling handfuls of red confetti into the air.
The bodies are gradually deposited about the stage.

MON   Nice one. Who's first?

LILY   Suzanne Porter.

MON   Yes.

(**SUZANNE PORTER** advances out of the shadows.)

LILY   One frosty November evening when the moon is full, a
hapless Suzanne Porter goes innocently . . .

MON   . . . to her doom . . .

LILY   . . . to her violin lesson. She pauses outside her violin
teacher's house and mentally rehearses her grade 12
standard Bruch concerto that she's been practising for
her Royal College of Music audition.

MON   She's completely unaware . . .

LILY   . . . that her violin teacher . . .

(**BARRY** advances.)

MON   The mild-mannered Mr Crabtree BA . . .

LILY   . . . LRCM . . .

MON   . . . in reality leads a double life as . . .

LILY   . . . the West Runton axe murderer. And tonight, as the full moon is full . . .

MON   . . . and he's run out of his normal medication . . .

LILY   . . . Suzanne Porter is about . . .

MON   . . . to get her strings tuned.

MR CRABTREE   Good evening, Suzanne. Come in.

SUZANNE   Hello, Mr Crabtree. Thank you.

MR CRABTREE   Come right through, Suzanne. I was just chopping some wood for the fire.

SUZANNE   Right.

(**We hear a violin being tuned as SUZANNE mimes. As CRABTREE attacks, the cast scream. Suzanne, with her back to the audience, throws red confetti into the air at the moment of impact. She falls backwards into the arms of BARRY and ALEX and is laid to rest, draped over the table.**)

LILY   And Lorraine Ferguson . . .

MON   . . . poor sad Lorraine Ferguson . . .

LILY   . . . makes her way to the saddling enclosure of the county's premier point to point.

(**LORRAINE 'mounts' her horse.**)

MON   . . . totally unaware that her horse . . .

LILY   . . . a handsome chestnut stallion called . . .

MON   . . . Conker . . .

LILY   . . . has been doped by the grooms of her jealous rivals.

MON   Nice one. His possetts have been laced with . . .

LILY   . . . the most potent hallucinogenic horse-drug known to veterinary science . . .

MON   . . . Equotrip!

LORRAINE   Bye, Mummy. Make sure you get a good photo of Conker taking the first water jump.

MON   At the first water jump, Conker, with a glint in his eye . . .

LILY   . . . and strands of foam flowing from his nostrils, is too fast for Mummy's polaroid. A fiery Pegasus . . .

MON   . . . as he leaps for the stars and keeps on going.

LILY   But Lorraine . . .

MON   . . . poor sad Lorraine, more mortal than her steed, tumbles to earth . . .

(As LORRAINE tumbles to earth in slow motion she is caught by BARRY.)

LILY   . . . landing on a carelessly placed spike.

ALEX produces a bloodied spike protruding from her back. The bell tolls. She is laid to rest. Confetti.)

And Caroline Pritchett . . .

(CAROLINE advances.)

MON   . . . collecting her J Reg Golf Automatic blah blah blah hatchback fuel-injected blah blah blah from her father's garage . . .

LILY   . . . fails to notice the grim and deadly set of the young mechanic's jaw.

CAROLINE   Thank you, Lennie. Is the car done?

LENNIE   Yes, Miss. I don't think she'll give you any more trouble.

CAROLINE   Great. Look, Lennie, I'm sorry that I laughed at you this morning when you asked me out, but the thought of us going out together was so ridiculous and . . . well, you weren't serious, were you?

LENNIE   No, Miss. I was just messing about.

CAROLINE   I thought so. You sounded so funny. I just couldn't help laughing.

LENNIE   That's alright, Miss. Only a joke. I should take the car for a good thrash on the bypass if I were you, Miss. Really put your foot down . . . See how she handles.

CAROLINE   Right. I'll do that. Thanks. Bye.

LENNIE   No, I don't think she'll give you any more trouble, Miss.

(The car is mimed. As CAROLINE turns the ignition key, the cast supply engine noise, gear change, etc. Caroline picks up speed and tries the brake. She panics as the car fails to respond. BARRY and ALEX surge in from behind her picking her up and rushing towards the audience as we hear the sound of impact and hear Caroline, with her arms across her face, screaming. The bell tolls. Confetti.)

LILY   And Gail Bentley . . .

MON   . . . poor dear Gail.

(GAIL advances.)

LILY   Actually, I don't mind Gail so much.

MON   No, she's not as bad as the others.

LILY   She'll actually talk to you, will Gail.

MON   Yeah . . . she's OK, is Gail.

LILY   Maybe we could spare her. Just break her legs in a skiing accident or something.

MON   Or she could go blind. Temporary blindness till after the play. It does happen.

LILY   Yeah . . . we could do that.

MON   Right.

LILY   *But* if we don't do the job properly there's always a chance . . .

MON   . . . the fates conspire . . .

LILY   . . . one thing leads to another . . .

MON   . . . and before you know where you are . . .

LILY   . . . Birnam Wood is on the move again. No, Mon, she's got to go.

MON   Sorry, Gail.

LILY   We had to do it.

MON   At the Duke of Edinburgh Awards hang-gliding for beginners weekend course . . .

LILY   . . . Gail Bentley nervously prepares for her first ascent.

(GAIL prepares her harness.)

INSTRUCTOR   OK, Gail. You've done your prelim checks. You're in your harness. How do you feel?

GAIL   I'm alright. I think I'm ready.

INSTRUCTOR   Right. Go to the edge and just start to trot down the slope.

(GAIL advances and is suddenly borne aloft by BARRY.)

INSTRUCTOR   Brilliant, Gail. Hold it steady. Left hand down. Shift your body weight. Left hand down.

LILY   But she can't.

GAIL   I can't.

LILY   She's paralysed by fear.

GAIL   I'm paralysed by fear.

LILY   She's gaining height.

GAIL   I'm gaining height.

INSTRUCTOR	Your left. Move to your left.
GAIL	I can't. I'm losing control. I'm going. Aaaaaagh!

(**The hang-glider crashes. GAIL is deposited. Red confetti. The bell.**)

LILY	And finally . . .
MON	Stephanie Boyce.

(**STEPHANIE advances.**)

LILY	The beautiful, intelligent, invulnerable, heavenly Stephanie . . .
MON	. . . number one contender for Lady Mac . . .
LILY	. . . goes swimming off the Great Barrier Reef . . .
MON	. . . whilst off on an Australian mini-break . . .
LILY	. . . paid for by her millionaire uncle.

(**STEPHANIE swims held horizontal by BARRY and ALEX.**)

MON	Professionally . . .
LILY	. . . with the economy of movement of a natural athlete . . .
MON	. . . she cleaves through the still blue waters . . .
LILY	. . . in her unbelievably sexy, purple one-piece . . .

(**We hear the** *Jaws* **music.**)

MON	From the deep . . .
LILY	. . . the arrow-slit eyes of a great white shark observe her rhythmic progress.
MON	And suddenly he strikes.

(**STEPHANIE screams, is jerked aloft by BARRY and ALEX and slowly, gracefully and sexily descends beneath the waves. Bell. Confetti. LILY and MON survey the carnage.**)

LILY	'I am one, my liege,

Whom the vile blows and buffets of the world
Have so incensed, that I am reckless what
I do, to spite the world.'

MON   Me too, Lil.

(**The bodies erupt into life as they speak their first line.**)

THE FIVE   (5) What we won't tolerate are the dumb (1) and dumpy
GIRLS   (2) the ugly (3) untrendy (4) girls with anoraks (5) and
funny-looking parents (1) with glasses (2) and no 0 levels
(3) girls who add nothing to our corporate (4) image and
appeal (1) girls (2) in short (3) who are naff (5) like Lily
Morgan.

(**The bell rings urgently as in a school playground and the FIVE
GIRLS return blankly and menacingly to their places. LILY
returns to the table and brushes aside the fallen confetti.**)

LILY   When we were in the first year this famous woman came
to talk to us in assembly. Do you remember, Mon?

MON   Um . . .

LILY   Oh come on, Mon, you must remember. She had been a
pupil at the school and now she was really successful.
She had her own business and she was supposed to be a
millionaire . . . a millionairess. She was very glamorous
and she'd got this amazing car outside in the car park
alongside all those funny little cars that the teachers
drive. She told us about flying to America and opening
new branches in Amsterdam and Paris and places like
that. She'd been on telly and everything. It was one of
these assemblies where everybody sits very still and
listens. And nobody coughs or shuffles about like they
always do when it's a vicar or police-dog handler or the
lady from the Spastics. It was totally still and silent. At
the end we were invited to ask questions and of course
nobody did. So the head said 'If you could attribute
your success to one single thing, what would it be?' And
this woman said . . .

MON   'If you want something badly enough and you're

prepared to work hard enough for it, then there's
nothing to stop you going out and getting it.'

LILY   Yes . . . that's it. You remembered. Everything's there
for the taking if you want it badly enough.

MON   Bollocks.

LILY   Yes . . . but what if it's true?

MON   True? Come on, Lily.

LILY   But what if it is? I've been thinking about that a lot these
last couple of days. What if it is true? Maybe the reason I
haven't had all the things I wanted was 'cos I didn't want
them badly enough. Maybe people get to be millionaires
and concert pianists and Olympic gold medallists . . .

MON   And Prime Minister, just because they want it more than
all the others. That's crap, Lily.

LILY   Why? Why is it? How do you know? Until you've
wanted something badly enough, how do you know?

MON   And what's badly enough, eh? Who measures 'badly
enough'? You think I don't want things? You think I
didn't want to be brilliant and tall and skinny and good
at Maths, eh? You think I don't look at Roland Masters
and long for him to come to me and say 'Monica, your
parents are going away for the weekend. Why don't
you . . .?' Do you think you're the only person to want
something badly enough? Do you think I'm me because
I want to be me?

LILY   I'm sorry . . . I'm sorry, Mon. I wasn't thinking.

MON   No.

LILY   Selfish.

MON   Yes.

LILY   I'm sorry.

MON   There you go again. Saying sorry. Being nice.

LILY   I know.

MON   Does she say sorry? Ever? Does she say sorry once in the whole play?

LILY   No.

MON   Does she hell . . . What time's your thing tomorrow?

LILY   1.30.

MON   Good luck.

LILY   You mean that, Mon?

MON   Bloody do it, Lil. (*They hug each other.*) Bloody do it.

(**Black out. Immediately in the darkness we hear STEPHANIE BOYCE's voice reading the speech 'I have given suck'. As the lights go up we see her advancing centre stage performing. LILY is watching intently, clutching a plastic carrier bag.**)

STEPHANIE   (*reading*) 'I have given suck and know
How tender 'tis to love the babe that milks me:
I would, while it was smiling in my face,
Have plucked my nipple from his boneless gums,
And dashed the brains out, had I so sworn
As you have done to this.'

MS BEVIS   Thank you, Stephanie. That was excellent. Well done. Very powerful. Good. OK . . . Lily. You still want to do this?

LILY   Yes.

MS BEVIS   Which bit do you want to read?

LILY   I'm not reading, Miss. I've learnt it.

MS BEVIS   Oh . . . Fine. Well, which speech do you want to do?

LILY   'Come you spirits that tend on mortal thoughts.'
(*The Five try to hide sniggers.*)

MS BEVIS   Right. Act I, Scene 5. OK. When you're ready.

(**LILY takes centre stage and removes a very sharp knife from her bag.**)

MS BEVIS   What have you got there, Lily?

LILY   Knife, Miss.

MS BEVIS   You need a prop, do you?

LILY   Yes.

MS BEVIS   Why?

LILY   It's got that bit about the keen knife . . . I've rehearsed it with a knife, Miss.

MS BEVIS   Well, OK. Be very careful, though. It looks very sharp.

LILY   Yes, it is, Miss. It's my brother's.

MS BEVIS   OK. Act I Scene 5 . . . Lady Macbeth with her brother's knife. (*sniggers from the Five*)

(LILY very solemnly comes downstage.)

LILY   'Come, you spirits
That tend on mortal thoughts, (*sniggers from the Five*)
unsex me here (*laughter*)
And fill me from the crown to the toe, top-full
Of direst cruelty!'

(She pauses and looks around at the FIVE GIRLS, who are desperately trying not to laugh. Her performance is still low key but quite chilling. Better than you'd have expected. This quality slowly spreads to the watching company. As the speech progresses they stop sniggering and start to look uneasy. LILY starts to play more and more with the knife and to play more directly to the Five.)

LILY   '. . . make thick my blood.
Stop up the access and passage to remorse;
That no compunctious visiting of nature
Shake my fell purpose . . .'

(She is now openly brandishing the knife.)

'Come to my woman's breasts . . .'

MS BEVIS   Lily, I don't think you should be wafting that knife around.

LILY   (*spinning on Ms Bevis*) 'Come to my WOMAN'S BREASTS,

And take my milk for gall, you murdering ministers,
Wherever in your sightless substances
You wait on nature's . . .'

MS BEVIS   Alright, Lily. Very good, But I really think that knife is a bit too dangerous to be . . .

LILY   'Come, thick night . . .'

MS BEVIS   Lily! Is this some kind of joke?

LILY   'And pall thee in the dunnest smoke of hell . . .'

MS BEVIS   Lily! I'm instructing you to put down that knife.

LILY   'That my keen knife . . .'

(She sits at the table, rolls up her sleeve and puts her naked left arm on the table.)

'. . . see not the wound it makes . . .'

(She raises the knife above her own arm.)

MS BEVIS   NO!

LILY   'Nor heaven peep through the blanket of the dark,
to cry . . .'

MS BEVIS   Someone fetch Mr Morris . . . Quickly!

LILY   Stay where you are! All of you.

(She looks around and smiles a sweet smile.)

Shall I stab or slash I wonder? It's so difficult to decide.
There's skin and tissue and tendons and bones and
somewhere . . . somewhere in there is a major artery . . .
I think.

MS BEVIS   Stop it, Lily . . . Please.

LILY   And it would sever and a little stub of purple pipe would
protrude and spurt and spurt. Is that alliteration, Miss,
or onomatopoeia. 'Yet who would have thought the old
man to have as much blood in him.' How high will it
spurt do you think?

MS BEVIS   Lily! Please!

LILY   'Here's the smell of blood still. All the perfumes of Arabia will not . . . Wash your hands, put on your night-gowns. Look not so pale. I tell you yet again, Banquo's buried. He cannot come out on's grave.'

(She screams. They all scream and hide their eyes as she plunges the knife into the table. The knife is left standing upright stuck into the table.)

Well, what did you think, Miss?

(LILY looks round at the group, who are shaken and open-mouthed. MS BEVIS is the first to move and she rushes forward to retrieve the knife.)

Miss, what did you think? All of you. Give me your honest opinion. (*Total silence. Long pause.*) Bit too much, perhaps? Bit over the top? Yeah, you're right . . . And they all just stood and stared, Mon. It was brilliant.

(MON appears.)

MON   What did she say?

LILY   Nothing. She just stared at me . . . Can I have the knife back, Miss? It's not mine. It's my brother's.

MS BEVIS   No . . . I don't think I'd better.

LILY   Come on, Miss . . . I was only acting. It's only me. I'm Lily for goodness sake.

MS BEVIS   Yes . . . well . . . I suppose it's alright.

LILY   Thanks. I'll put it in its sheath. For safety. Well, thanks for hearing me, Miss. Could I put my name down for costumes?

MS BEVIS   What?

LILY   I'd like to help out with costumes.

MS BEVIS   What?

LILY   Or make-up. Something backstage.

MS BEVIS   But I thought you wanted to . . .

LILY   No, not really. Not my thing really. Not my style. Come on, be honest. You can't really see me as Lady Macbeth, can you, Miss. And incidentally, I thought Stephanie Boyce was brilliant. Really powerful. Didn't you? What did you think, Miss?

MS BEVIS   Yes . . . she was . . . very good.

LILY   Really brilliant. By the way, Miss, how are you thinking of costuming this?

MS BEVIS   Pardon?

LILY   What sort of costumes for *Macbeth*?

MS BEVIS   Oh . . . Jacobean Gothic . . . I thought.

LILY   Nice one. I'll start doing some research on that.

MS BEVIS   Yes . . . Fine . . . Thank you.

LILY   (*smiles*) And now they'll say . . .

THE FIVE   (1) It was really embarrassing (2) She'd brought this knife (3) and, she started brandishing it about (4) Pretended to threaten to stab herself (5) Indulgent (1) Did she think Bevis was going to cast her after that? (2) after that display (3) We were wetting ourselves (4) It was hilarious (5) It was so funny (1) I thought I was going to die.

MOTHER   I told you, didn't I? Water off a duck's back. A girl like Lily's got to be realistic. You've got to get used to disappointment in this life and Lily knows that better than anybody.

BARRY   Oh, don't get me wrong. I admire you for having a go, but . . . Well, it wasn't you really, Lily. And costumes, now, that's a really vital area, I should think.

ALEX   I've volunteered to paint scenery, Lil, me and Kev. We were up there on ladders all lunchtime looking down Stephanie Boyce's blouse. She's amazing, Lil. Really talented. 'Come, you spirits that tend on mortal thoughts, unsex me here.' Amazing. Don't know what it means but it sounds sort of kinky when Stephanie says it.

MS BEVIS The problem is the girls. They don't seem to be developing any power. It's almost as if they were holding back. Inhibited. And Lily's there at every rehearsal, looming largely at the back, with her measuring tape and a large pair of scissors.

LILY Just in case anything needs adjusting, Miss.

MS BEVIS And they look at her and they seem to shrink. It's quite extraordinary how they've shrunk.

MON Why, Lily? I don't understand. Why did you do that? I mean you wanted to play her . . . didn't you?

LILY I played her, Mon.

MON And that was enough?.

LILY Yeah . . . it was enough . . . for the time being.

(Solo voice singing 'Lavender's Blue'. Blackout.)

WRITING THE PLAY

I sometimes find when I'm trying to write that my ideas won't do what they're told. They seem to have a mind of their own.

Not long ago I was involved in directing a youth theatre festival which consisted of four shortened versions of Shakespeare's plays. I was very interested and quite surprised to find that even though there were lots of parts for girls (one of the plays was to be an all-female production), the one which easily created the most interest and the fiercest competition in audition was Lady Macbeth, arguably the most evil woman that Shakespeare ever created. Everybody, it seemed, wanted to be Lady Macbeth. I wondered why this might be and decided it might be an interesting idea for a play.

Around the same time I read somewhere that there are about forty times more men than women in British prisons. Again I found myself asking why this might be. Are women by nature less likely than men to commit crimes or does something happen to them as they grow up which prevents them from breaking the law? Is it somehow harder for girls than for boys to do wrong or is it just lack of opportunity? I decided I'd write a play about this too.

As I started scribbling down notes for the two plays I found that the two ideas kept bumping together, and however hard I tried I couldn't separate them. I slowly realised what I should have known all along: the two ideas belonged together and what I had was one play, not two. I started again and wrote *Living with Lady Macbeth*.

The first decision I made when writing *Living with Lady Macbeth* was that the setting would not be a school or a house or a street but simply an open space which could become instantly any of these, and many more, simply by the words which the characters spoke. If you believe that theatre audiences, like readers, are capable of using their imaginations, then it's not necessary to show them precise details surrounding every scene. If you give them the right clues the audience will do the rest.

Once I'd decided this, I found that Lily could flash backwards and forwards in time. She could remember bits of conversations she'd had with her mum, with Barry, her boyfriend, or with her teacher, Ms Bevis. She could listen in on people's conversations, show us her dreams and even allow us to watch as she 'kills off' her enemies in her imagination.

Finally, I'd like to thank the original cast of *Living with Lady Macbeth*. Not only were they a talented young company but they also felt strongly about their characters and were not afraid to tell me when they thought I'd got something wrong. They'd often say things like 'I don't like this bit. I don't think she'd say this.' I would ask them what they would prefer to say. Invariably they'd be right.

FOLLOW-UP ACTIVITIES

In *Living with Lady Macbeth* the narrative (the story-line) moves between the world of Shakespeare's *Macbeth* and the world of Lily, an ordinary-seeming schoolgirl, who has decided to audition for the part of Lady Macbeth in a school production of the play.

Some of the activities that follow are concerned with *Living with Lady Macbeth*, while others are connected with Shakespeare's tragedy. If your main interest lies in *Living with Lady Macbeth*, you may decide to omit some of the activities that relate to *Macbeth*. However, if you've never seen Shakespeare's play, this may be a good opportunity to do so. There may be a theatre production locally, or you may be able to get a video copy of a performance. It's an exciting play to read, with plenty of intrigue, action and suspense. The drama includes superstition and the supernatural, treason, battles, guilt and murder.

Drama ideas

The structure of *Living with Lady Macbeth* is very close to the improvisation that you might use in a drama studio. The characters often go from one time and place to another (and back again) as quickly as between one scripted line and the next. The action does not use real time or realistic scenery. The playwright notes in his discussion 'Writing the Play' that he quite deliberately chose to set the action on an empty stage so that the space could instantly become anything that the actors and the audience might want it to be. This puts a lot of responsibility on the actors to make sure that the situation is as clear as possible for the audience who, in their turn, have to imagine the place where the activity is set.

- In a small group of three or four people, choose a scene from *Living with Lady Macbeth* which has a specific setting – perhaps a classroom, or Lily's home. Work on staging the scene so that, without using any scenery, you can give a sense of the situation. Do people move differently, sit differently in classrooms, and homes? How do different people use the spaces? What, for example, is Lily's mother doing as she speaks with her daughter? And, in her turn, what is Lily doing?

If there are more people in your group than parts you might like to try to find a way of including everyone.

- In the same group, turn your attention to the opening scene of *Macbeth*. The play gives very little instruction as to how this scene with the three witches may be played, other than suggesting an open place accompanied by thunder and lightning. Try and make the scene as atmospheric as you can. In a production you might use electronic sound, lighting and stage effects. For this exercise, however, try using voices and movement to create the necessary effects, in the simple and direct style of *Living with Lady Macbeth*.

In putting together a dramatic presentation, there is often a lot of exploration, rehearsal and refinement of ideas that has to happen before the cast, company and director feel that it works well and achieves what has been aimed for. Although a playwright might give detailed staging instructions, these do not have to be followed and you may well have other ideas that will work as effectively. For instance, in *Living with Lady Macbeth* Rob John suggests that red confetti be used to symbolise blood in the imagined death scenes of the five schoolgirls. It's a small detail but one that you might want to change. Remember all those jokes about tomato sauce!

- Choose one of the scenes in the script that deals with Mon and Lily's imagined sticky ends for the five girls. In your group, work on two different versions of the scene.

Firstly, follow the scripted stage instructions as closely as you can. You may not have props to hand, such as the red confetti, but you could improvise with newspaper or mime. It will help if you can become familiar enough with the lines to be able to put your books down – don't worry about being word perfect.

In the second version, free yourself totally from the writer's instructions and plan your own dramatisation of the scene. Explore different ways of showing someone playing a violin, riding a horse, driving a car. Try this using only people's bodies, voices and movements and no props at all. You can have as much fun as you like with this, since the writing is witty and the whole sequence invites the actors to be funny. It is sometimes difficult with comedy to prevent humour from becoming silliness. You might like to show your rehearsed scene to an audience and ask them to decide whether you've remained on the right side of the line which divides the two.

- In the middle of all the intrigue and tragedy of *Macbeth*, there is a scene (Act II, Scene 3) whose beginning is often staged comically. This lightens the mood for a while, though the tension is restored as soon as Macbeth enters. Have a look at this first part of the scene – it may be worth sorting out any words or expressions that you are unfamiliar with before beginning the dramatisation of the scene.

See if you can stage this scene in a lively and interesting way, using only voices and movement.

A playscript offers the basic material for a performance. A play is not dramatic until actors lift it from a page and give it an active and dynamic form. Although the playwright's words are always of great importance, actors often develop a part by careful use of expression, movement and turning. This is why we have expressions such as a 'pause for dramatic effect'. Theatre critics, writing in newspaper columns, are often concerned with an actor's or director's interpretation of a particular role. Is Macbeth a weak man? Is Macbeth corrupted by the greed for power, or manipulated by his wife? Is Macbeth, like a figure from a Greek tragedy, set on a course by fate (the witches' predictions) from which he cannot escape? Is Lady Macbeth fired by the possibility of being queen or serving the cause of her husband? These are all questions which may be answered – or left open – by the way in which an actor or director decides a part should be played. The following activities are intended to help you explore different ways of interpreting a particular scene.

- With a partner, work on a series of quick, short tableaux

(frozen moments) that might show the following attitudes:

confidence   disdain
laughter   fear
suspicion   anger
pleasure   panic

You might like to show these to an audience and discuss with them the differences between each emotion. Some are quite distinct, but others are quite closely related. For instance, it may be quite difficult to physically express the difference between fear and panic.

- At one point in *Living with Lady Macbeth*, Lily muses about the five girls. She suggests that she can judge what they are saying by their physical attitudes: 'On a wall by the edge of the park they sit. Lunchtimes in the summer. They show their legs and men mowing the grass whistle. They giggle and smoke. I know what they're saying . . . You can tell from a distance . . . By the way they sit . . . By the way they hold their necks and their arms and their hands and the way they blow their smoke. They're saying . . .'

  In the scene, the girls go on to say things. Yet Lily cannot hear this or know what it is that is said. She judges from their physical attitudes. Using mime, see if a group of you can stage this scene on the wall so that your audience can clearly imagine the sort of conversation that is being conducted.

- In Act III, Scene 4 of *Macbeth*, Macbeth and Lady Macbeth entertain at a banquet. During the course of the meal, Macbeth's guilt turns to terror as he is visited by the ghost of Banquo (a general murdered at Macbeth's command in order that his sons should not succeed Macbeth, as had been predicted by the three witches). None of the other guests can see this apparition and it is suggested that Macbeth is either unwell or having a fit. First, read the scene closely and discuss both what is happening and how you understand what is happening. Then, using mime, try staging this scene offering your interpretations of what the guests, Macbeth and Lady Macbeth are thinking and feeling. What are their different reactions? How can these be expressed physically? How can you get the audience to understand Macbeth's fear and Lady

Macbeth's attempts to hold the party together? How can you show the guests' reactions, which will probably include confusion, alarm or suspicion?

Often, when we want someone to do something, we will go about it in a very indirect manner. You can probably think of any number of examples in your own lives such as talking too loudly about your birthday a few days before the event or explaining to a teacher that some other member of staff does things in a different manner. Barry, in *Living with Lady Macbeth*, suggests that Lily has taken on too much: 'I don't know how you think you're going to find the time to do your studying . . . and this play . . . and see me. Something'll have to go. And another thing, Lily. You've started acting very oddly since this whole business started. *Very* oddly, in my opinion.'

What is it that Barry wants Lily to give up? And why is he so indirect in his discussion?

- With a partner improvise a scene where one of you has her/his eyes 'fixed on the shadow of her[his] solitary ambition'.

  The other wants to persuade their partner to give up that ambition, but doesn't feel able to say so directly, and so has to find indirect ways of making the point.

- In *Living with Lady Macbeth*, Lily is very aware of how other people perceive her. She rarely confronts them with their judgements and often simply plays along with whatever is said. Her mother describes Lily as 'very ordinary really' and the teacher sees her as 'a real trier. Not overbright.'

  With a partner work on one of the speeches (pp.11–13) these quotations are taken from. One of you plays Lily's mother or Ms Bevis, the other plays Lily herself. Explore ways of letting Lily strike back and contradict the statements made. What effect does this have on her mother or her teacher?

- Look at Act I, Scene 7 in *Macbeth*, where Macbeth expresses his uncertainty about the plan to kill Duncan. How does Lady Macbeth persuade her husband that he should still go ahead with the plot? With a partner and using your own words, improvise a scene that explores different ways that Macbeth may answer his wife's judgements of him. Can he keep his loyalty to Duncan, please Lady Macbeth or change the course of her ambitions, and still maintain his self-respect?

Design

In the stage directions at the beginning of *Living with Lady Macbeth* it is suggested that Macbeth is to be seen as a 'traditionally costumed figure' who is 'obviously Shakespearean' and 'clearly Scottish'. What tradition do you think the playwright is referring to in this direction? Is he referring to the costume that may have been worn in Shakespeare's own lifetime in the theatre? Is it a reference to the firmly established customs of Victorian and Edwardian theatre's approach to Shakespeare? What does it mean to appear 'clearly Scottish'?

• Find out about some productions of *Macbeth* from the past and see if you can find pictures or descriptions of costumes that you feel may be appropriate. Try to find books that carry illustrations of famous actors in the role of Macbeth. Use your own research to help you design a costume (rather than simply copying one) for your own production of *Living with Lady Macbeth*. Remember to include elements which are 'traditional', 'Shakespearean' and 'Scottish' and try to avoid overdressing or too much fussy detail.

• The five schoolgirls appear on stage in their school uniforms. Rather than using an existing school uniform for your costumes, try designing your own. What is it that makes a school uniform recognisable and distinguishable from the uniform of an airline steward or a staff member of a department store? Draw sketches of details and the overall appearance. You might also like to collect fabric samples and work out a budget. Think about all the costumes for your production. Is it possible to make some element (for example of colour or design) common to all of them?

Discussion

According to Rob John one of the things that prompted him to write this play was the discovery that there are almost forty times more men than women in prisons. Of course, there will be many reasons for this and they will not necessarily be because women commit fewer crimes than men. However, the question that this raises for the playwright is whether there is some essential difference between the sexes, or whether this startling fact has its cause in the different ways in which society sees men and women. At least one educational researcher suggests that commonly held views on the respective abilities of boys and girls are dangerous. For instance, she says that a survey of males and females in mathematics did not prove the differences of talent that are usually suggested. What it did reveal was prejudice in teachers. If girls performed badly, the teachers could not ever consider them any good at the subject. If boys performed badly, the teachers tended to believe that they had hidden qualities.[1] Lily's teacher may be making just such a judgement when she suggests that Lily 'reached her peak at GCSE'. You might like to give the question of what people expect of males and females some thought and discuss it in a group.

- Lily's mother calls Stephanie Boyce 'a proper little madam'. What does this expression mean to you? List as many other sayings that you can think of which are often used to describe people ('a right little so and so', 'a good for nothing'). Can they be sorted by gender, and if so, which is the longer list? Discuss the different expressions and whether you think they are fair descriptions of people or whether they relate to prejudices people hold about the way men and women behave.

- Lily, when she is describing what it is that Lady Macbeth does to provoke Macbeth to commit the murder of Duncan, says 'So I insult his manhood'. This happens in *Macbeth* Act I Scene 7, where Lady Macbeth comments:

[1] Valerie Walkerdine, *Femininity as Performance in Schoolgirl Fictions* (Verso, 1991), pp. 134–5.

When you durst do it, then you were a man;
And, to be more than what you were, you would
Be so much more the man.

Discuss what it is that Lady Macbeth sees as 'being a man'.
Do you think she is right? How does she see her role as a
woman? She says, for instance:

I have given suck, and know
How tender 'tis to love the babe that milks me:
I would, while it was smiling in my face,
Have plucked my nipple from his boneless gums,
And dashed the brains out, had I so sworn
As you have done to this.

- Barry suggests that Lily cannot play Lady Macbeth because
  she is 'too nice'. In much the same way, Lady Macbeth
  worries whether her husband can realise his ambition to be
  king because he is:

  . . . too full of the milk of human kindness
  To catch the nearest way.

  As a group, you may like to discuss whether success and
  ambition are necessarily connected with ruthlessness? Does
  kindness and gentleness have no part in achievement? Do you
  think kindness and gentleness are qualities that belong to a
  particular gender?

- In most Western countries, doctors are considered to be
  members of a high-status profession. In the USSR, doctors
  have relatively low status. In Western countries, the majority
  of doctors are men. In the USSR, the majority of doctors are
  women.

  You may like to consider this fact, and discuss whether
  women entering what have been traditionally male jobs are
  changing the narrow ways people have tended to think about
  men's and women's roles. Or do people use their entrenched
  attitudes to pass judgement on women in the new situations
  in which they find themselves? If so, how can this be
  changed?